BÉABA

BABY COOK® BOOK

Babycook® Book

New Edition: Recipes for a Healthy Eater

Contributing Author: Yvette Saulnier
Photography: Tanya J. Blum

Publisher's Warning and Disclaimer:

All content in this book is for informational purposes only and should not be construed as medical advice or instruction. You should always consult your pediatrician before introducing new foods to your baby. For further nutritional information, contact the American Academy of Pediatrics.

The recipes in this book feature "recommended" age indications, starting from the age of 5 months. We remind you that introducing new foods into a baby's diet must be carried out under the supervision of a pediatrician who is in a position to adapt nutritional diversification to each child, taking into account the possible risk of allergies or other concerns.

The information in this book is offered with no guarantees and no representations or warranties as to its accuracy or completeness. We disclaim all liability and warranties in connection with the use of this book, including but not limited to, any warranties of merchantability or fitness for a particular purpose, whether express or implied by law, course of dealing, course of performance, usage of trade or otherwise.

Design by Gustavo Stecher, Menos es Mas

Babycook is a registered trademark of Peek A Boo USA, Inc.

© 2016, Peek A Boo USA, Inc.
ISBN 978-0-692-67086-6

Table of Contents
–

5+ MONTHS

Baby's First:
Meal ideas for the new eater

8+ MONTHS

Beyond Basics:

Combining flavors for a developing palette

12+ MONTHS

Growing Baby:

Meal ideas for a growing appetite

18+ MONTHS

Little Tikes:

Tasty toddler meals

FAMILY

Beyond Baby:

Prenatal, postnatal and family recipes

Nutritional Variety

New food, flavors, and nutritional benefits for the beginning eater.

Needs and quantities change at every stage.

Your baby is growing. His needs are changing, so foods, as well as quantities, must be adapted. Fluctuations in baby's food intake can be alarming for a parent or caregiver. One day a baby may eat everything offered, and the next day, not so much. In the background, there's a looming fear of not feeding your baby correctly. Don't worry! Rest assured that you and your baby will fall into a rhythm with solid food just as you did with the breast or bottle. Here is a handy guide to approximately how much a baby should be eating each day, according to age and type of food.

In practice:

A baby is not the same as an adult in terms of nutritional needs and taste. Babies don't consider that their yogurts aren't "glamorous" enough, or that their purées are "tasteless." Trust your baby's ability to regulate his intake, both in terms of likes and disikes and in the amount consumed. In most cases, a child will eat exactly as much food as he needs. Suggested serving sizes are designed to reassure parents, but you should trust your baby to self-regulate. A baby's food needs will fluctuate from one day to another; this is normal, sometimes he will be hungry, and sometimes he will be reluctant to eat. Your baby will pace himself over several days. There is no need to worry as long as his weight is within the normal standard.

Weaning:

Weaning refers to the transition from breast-feeding to bottle-feeding or from bottle-feeding to nutritional variety. Whenever you choose to wean your baby, it can be an emotional time (some mamas may be happy to begin a new chapter, while others may feel sad over losing the close connection breast-feeding can foster). Weaning means that your baby is growing and getting older and growing more independent. The baby will need to be reassured that he's still safe, even though he may be losing the closeness of breast or bottle-feeding.

Dads and other family members or caregivers can play an important role in making a smooth transition from exclusive nursing and the bottle to solid foods. Having other family members or your baby's caregiver feed your baby allows the "feeding link" to expand beyond mom. It can also give mom a much-needed break.

Weaning for the mom:

For the best possible experience, mom should focus on the benefits of weaning - and there are loads of benefits. The baby will gain new autonomy, and the mom will regain hims. If she's breast-feeding, she'll take back possession of her own body. She'll be able to refocus on her relationships with her spouse or partner, her colleagues, and her social circle. She'll also be able to share the role of nurturing her child with others. Her role with her child will also change, and the shift will allow her to accompany the child as he learns and discovers the world, enabling him to break the exclusive link that is breast-feeding.

Weaning in practice:

The baby's father, caregivers, or other supportive family members can help support the transition in the following ways:

- Gradually spacing bottle-feedings.
- Taking over bottle-feedings.
- Mixing the milk (breast milk and formula or breast milk and cow's milk) so that baby can get used to the new taste.
- Finding the right temperature for the milk or the meal.
- Allowing mom to be in another room or doing something else during the meal, so that the baby does not "feel" the presence of mom and can more readily accept new foods.
- Helping the child feel secure by fulfilling the baby's nutritional needs.

Why is nutritional variety important?

For a baby, nutritional variety is a way to move forward and discover the world. In tasting different foods and stimulating his taste buds, a baby can start building up her own list of food preferences. In general, when approached with gentleness and respect for the baby's rhythm, the transition is well received.

At this stage, the parent should be focused on ensuring nutritional variety, an important aspect of raising a healthy, growing baby. By introducing your food culture, you are offering an education and sharing taste sensations that allow your baby to learn his palette. And you, in turn, begin to discover the little eater in front of you.

In practice:

Start introducing nutritional variety in the comfort of your home, rather than at a restaurant. Being at home in a familiar environment will help you and your baby relax. It's also important for you to be able to focus on your baby, to observe your baby's facial expressions, and reactions to these new tastes. Praise him for his successes. Reassure him if he doesn't want to try something new; if it's not today, it will be another day. Don't place too much importance on these experiments. Successful or not, there's plenty of time for both of you to get there. Be ready to watch your baby become an empowered eater.

BABY FEEDING GUIDE

5+ MONTHS

banana, orange, plum, peach, apricot

apple, pear, grape

carrot, broccoli, beet, sweet potato

green beans, squash, tomato, avocado

yogurt, soft cheeses

egg yolk (hard-boiled)

butter, oil (except nut oil)

baby cereal

8+ MONTHS

pineapple, melon, kiwi, mango

spinach, cauliflower, sweet pepper

asparagus, eggplant, celery, peas

onion, mushroom, lentils, beans

cod, sea bass, sole, salmon, poultry

ham, red meat

potato, pasta, rice, grains, bread

12+ MONTHS

cow´s milk

berries*

exotic fruit

pork

whole egg (hard boiled)**

honey*

18+ MONTHS

scallops, shellfish*

nuts or nut oils*

chocolate*

pickles, raw vegetables

cabbage, radish, beans

*All foods should be cooked unless stated otherwise. Pay special attention for potential allergic reactions when serving these foods. Meat, poultry, seafood and other cooked foods should be cooked to a safe minimum internal temperature. See www.foodsafety.gov for safe minimum internal cooking temperatures (United States). In Canada please see: http://healthycanadians.gc.ca/eating-nutrition/safety-salubrite/cook-temperatures-cuisson-eng.php. The above information is for general guidance only. Each child is different. You should consult your child's physician or pediatrician prior to introducing new foods or for questions regarding food safety and your child.

Congratulations!

You now own a Babycook® – a unique appliance that will allow you to steam cook, blend, reheat, and defrost delicious homemade meals for your baby and the whole family. Babycook was created on the notion that making homemade baby food should be simple, easy and can even be fun. Everything you'll need to make healthy food for your baby, from the first bite onward, is contained in this single appliance.

The recipes included in this book were created specifically for use with the Babycook appliance and take between 5 to 15 minutes to cook, depending on the dish. Once you get the hang of using the Babycook with the recipes in this cookbook, you may want to branch out and create your own recipes.

When appropriate, you'll find helpful information at the start of each recipe with cooking time and water level. On the left side of the Babycook blending bowl, you will see graduation marks from 1 to 3; these levels help you measure the amount of water to be poured into the heating reservoir and determine the amount of time it will take for your food to steam cook.

Baby's First:

Meal ideas for the new eater

5+	MONTHS

BÉABA

BABYCOOK® BOOK

5+ MONTHS

Green Bean Purée

 PREP TIME
5 min

COOK TIME
10 min

WATER
Level 2

Ingredients:

2 - 3 cups green beans, or whatever quantity fills the steamer basket

Steps:

Put the green beans in the steamer basket.
Pour water into the tank (level 2).
Start the cooking process.
When the green beans are cooked, put them in the blending bowl and set aside the cooking liquid.
Blend, adding some of the cooking liquid to bring the purée to the desired consistency.
Serve immediately. You may also store in Béaba storage containers refrigerated up to 3 days or freeze.

Foodie Fact

Green beans are a great starter food because their gentle fibers are well tolerated by baby's tummy.

5+ MONTHS

Zucchini Purée

PREP TIME
5 min

COOK TIME
15 min

WATER
Level 3

Ingredients:

Steps:

2 – 3 cups cubed zucchini, or whatever quantity fills the steamer basket

Put the zucchini in the steamer basket.
Pour water into the tank (level 3).
Start the cooking process.
When the zucchini is cooked, put it in the blending bowl and set aside the cooking liquid.
Blend, adding some of the cooking liquid to bring the purée to the desired consistency.
Serve immediately. You may also store in Béaba storage containers refrigerated up to 3 days or freeze.

🔍 *Foodie Fact* ——————

Zucchini is rich in magnesium, which is good for regulating baby's intestinal track. It's also loaded with vitamins A, B-Complex, E and K.

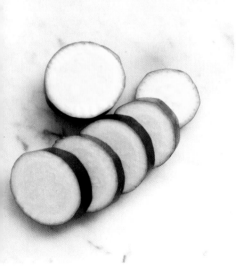

5+ MONTHS

Butternut Squash Purée

PREP TIME
5 min

COOK TIME
15 min

WATER
Level 3

Ingredients:

Steps:

2 - 3 cups cubed butternut squash, or whatever quantity fills the steamer basket

Foodie Fact

The slightly sweet and chest-nutty flavor of butternut squash is a favorite for baby. It's also rich in vitamins A and C.

Put the squash in the steamer basket.
Pour water into the tank (level 3).
Start the cooking process.
When the squash is cooked, put it in the blending bowl and set aside the cooking liquid.
Blend, adding some of the cooking liquid to bring the purée to the desired consistency.
Serve immediately. You may also store in Béaba storage containers refrigerated up to 3 days or freeze.

5+ MONTHS

Broccoli Purée

PREP TIME
5 min

COOK TIME
15 min

WATER
Level 3

Ingredients:

2 – 3 cups broccoli florets, or whatever quantity fills the steamer basket

Steps:

Put the broccoli in the steamer basket.
Pour water into the tank (level 3).
Start the cooking process.
When the broccoli is cooked, put it in the blending bowl and set aside the cooking liquid.
Blend, adding some of the cooking liquid to bring the purée to the desired consistency.
Serve immediately. You may also store in Béaba storage containers refrigerated up to 3 days or freeze.

🔍 *Foodie Fact* ───────
Broccoli tastes sweet when cooked and baby will love the green color. It's also rich in vitamins C, K, and B9.

5+ MONTHS

Carrot Purée

PREP TIME
5 min

COOK TIME
15 min

WATER
Level 3

Ingredients:

2 - 3 cups sliced carrots, or
whatever quantity fills the
steamer basket

Steps:

Put the carrots in the steamer basket.
Pour water into the tank (level 3).
Start the cooking process.
When the carrots are cooked, put them in the blending bowl and set aside
the cooking liquid.
Blend, adding some of the cooking liquid to bring the purée to the desired
consistency.
*Serve immediately. You may also store in Béaba storage containers
refrigerated up to 3 days or freeze.*

Foodie Fact

*Carrots are a great source of
calcium, which helps baby
build healthy bones.*

5+ MONTHS

Pumpkin Purée

⌣ PREP TIME
5 min

⌚ COOK TIME
15 min

◌ WATER
Level 3

Ingredients:

2 – 3 cups cubed pumpkin, or whatever quantity fills the steamer basket

Steps:

Put the pumpkin in the steamer basket.
Pour water into the tank (level 3).
Start the cooking process.
When the pumpkin is cooked, put it in the blending bowl and set aside the cooking liquid.
Blend, adding some of the cooking liquid to bring the purée to the desired consistency.
Serve immediately. You may also store in Béaba storage containers refrigerated up to 3 days or freeze.

🔍 *Foodie Fact*

Pumpkins are a great source of magnesium, which can have a calming effect on babies with colic.

5+ MONTHS

Apple
Purée

PREP TIME
5 min

COOK TIME
10 min

WATER
Level 2

Ingredients:

**2 - 3 cups cubed apples, or
whatever quantity fills the
steamer basket**

Steps:

Put the apples in the steamer basket.
Pour water into the tank (level 2).
Start the cooking process.
When the apples are cooked, put them in the blending
bowl and set aside the cooking liquid.
Blend, adding some of the cooking liquid to bring the
purée to the desired consistency.
*Serve immediately. You may also store in Béaba
storage containers refrigerated up to 3 days or freeze.*

Foodie Fact

*Pectin, a fiber found in apples, transforms into
a gel during digestion, which makes them easy
on baby's tummy.*

5+ MONTHS

Pear Purée

PREP TIME
5 min

COOK TIME
10 min

WATER
Level 2

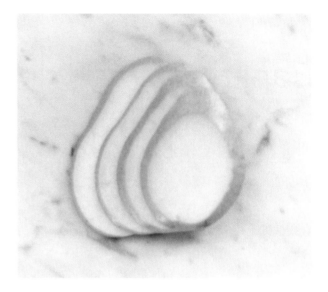

Ingredients:

2 - 3 cups cubed pears, or whatever quantity fills the steamer basket

Steps:

Put the pears in the steamer basket.
Pour water into the tank (level 2).
Start the cooking process.
When the pears are cooked, put them in the blending bowl and set aside the cooking liquid.
Blend, adding some of the cooking liquid to bring the purée to the desired consistency.
Serve immediately. You may also store in Béaba storage containers refrigerated up to 3 days or freeze.

🔍 *Foodie Fact*

Pears provide a similar fiber to apples. The graininess offers an opportunity to introduce a new texture to baby.

5+ MONTHS

Banana Purée

PREP TIME
5 min

COOK TIME
10 min

WATER
Level 2

Ingredients:

Steps:

2 - 3 cups sliced bananas, or whatever quantity fills the steamer basket

Put the bananas in the steamer basket.
Pour water into the tank (level 2).
Start the cooking process.
When the bananas are cooked, put them in the blending bowl and set aside the cooking liquid.
Blend, adding some of the cooking liquid to bring the purée to the desired consistency.
Serve immediately. You may also store in Béaba storage containers refrigerated up to 3 days or freeze.

Foodie Fact

Bananas are a great source of potassium for baby. Potassium is important for muscle function and for heart health.

5+ MONTHS

Plum Purée

◠ PREP TIME
5 min

◔ COOK TIME
15 min

◇ WATER
Level 3

Ingredients:

2 - 3 cups sliced plums, or whatever quantity fills the steamer basket

Steps:

Put the plums in the steamer basket.
Pour water into the tank (level 3).
Start the cooking process.
When the plums are cooked, put them in the blending bowl and set aside the cooking liquid.
Blend, adding some of the cooking liquid to bring the purée to the desired consistency.
Serve immediately. You may also store in Béaba storage containers refrigerated up to 3 days or freeze.

🔍 *Foodie Fact*
Plums are a great source of fiber for baby. To reduce the laxative effect, mix them with another fruit like apples or bananas.

5+ MONTHS

Seedless Grape Purée

PREP TIME
5 min

COOK TIME
10 min

WATER
Level 2

Ingredients:

Steps:

2 - 3 cups seedless grapes, or whatever quantity fills the steamer basket

Foodie Fact

Red or darker skinned grapes contain more antioxidants than green grapes. Be sure to steam and puree as whole grapes are a choking hazard for very young babies.

Put the grapes in the steamer basket.
Pour water into the tank (level 2).
Start the cooking process.
When the grapes are cooked, put them in the blending bowl and set aside the cooking liquid.
Blend, adding some of the cooking liquid to bring the purée to the desired consistency
Serve immediately. You may also store in Béaba storage containers refrigerated up to 3 days or freeze.

5+ MONTHS

Sweet Potato and Carrot Purée

PREP TIME
5 min

COOK TIME
15 min

WATER
Level 3

Ingredients:

1 cup cubed sweet potatoes
1 cup cubed carrots

Steps:

Put the potatoes and carrots in the steamer basket.
Pour water into the tank (level 3).
Start the cooking process.
When the vegetables are cooked, put them in the blending bowl and set aside the cooking liquid.
Blend, adding some of the cooking liquid to bring the purée to the desired consistency.
Serve immediately. You may also store in Béaba storage containers refrigerated up to 3 days or freeze.

Foodie Fact ————————————

Carrots and sweet potatoes combined provide more than 100% of the daily recommended vitamin A, which promotes healthy eyes, skin and immune system.

5+ MONTHS

Beet and Apple Purée

PREP TIME	5 min
COOK TIME	15 min
WATER	Level 3

Ingredients:

**1 cup cubed red beets
(raw or cooked)
1 cup cubed apple**

Steps:

Put the beets and apples in the steamer basket.
Pour water into the tank (level 3).
Start the cooking process.
When the apples and beets are cooked, put them in
the blending bowl and set aside the cooking liquid.
Blend, adding some of the cooking liquid to bring the
purée to the desired consistency.
*Serve immediately. You may also store in Béaba
storage containers refrigerated up to 3 days
or freeze.*

Foodie Fact

*The sugary taste of beets and apples makes this dish
an easy transition from milk or formula to vegetables.*

Beyond Basics:

Combining flavors for a developing palette

8+	MONTHS

BÉABA

BABYCOOK® BOOK

8+ MONTHS

Autumn Chicken

 PREP TIME
5 min

COOK TIME
15 min

WATER
Level 3

Ingredients:

2 cups cubed butternut squash
1 cup cubed potato
1 ounce cubed chicken breast
1 teaspoon olive oil

> 🔍 *Foodie Fact* —————
> *Chicken is a great source of lean protein for baby. Plus, butternut squash adds gentle fiber for a healthy tummy.*

Steps:

Put the squash, potato, and chicken in the steamer basket.
Pour water into the tank (level 3).
Start the cooking process.
When the vegetables and chicken are cooked, put them in the blending bowl and set aside the cooking liquid.
Blend, adding 1 teaspoon of olive oil and some of the cooking liquid to bring to the desired consistency.
Serve immediately. You may also store in Béaba storage containers refrigerated up to 3 days or freeze.

8+ MONTHS

Garden Zucchini Chicken

PREP TIME
5 min

COOK TIME
15 min

WATER
Level 3

Ingredients:

1 ½ cups cubed zucchini
½ cup cubed potato
1 ounce cubed chicken breast

1 pat of butter
Dill to taste (optional)

Steps:

Put the zucchini, potato, and chicken in the steamer basket.
Pour water into the tank (level 3).
Start the cooking process.
When the vegetables and chicken are cooked, put them in the blending bowl and set aside the cooking liquid.
Blend, adding the pat of butter and some of the cooking liquid to bring to the desired consistency.
If desired, add a small amount of dill and blend.
Serve immediately. You may also store in Béaba storage containers refrigerated up to 3 days or freeze.

🔍 *Foodie Fact*
Potatoes are easy to digest and provide baby with energy and B vitamins. They blend well with other foods and add a creamy texture to purées.

8+ MONTHS

Cider Pork and Potatoes

PREP TIME
5 min

COOK TIME
15 min

WATER
Level 3

Ingredients:

1 cup cubed sweet potato
1 cup cubed apple
1 ounce cubed pork tenderloin

1 teaspoon olive oil
Pinch of cinnamon (optional)

Steps:

Put the sweet potato, apple, and pork in the steamer basket.
Pour water into the tank (level 3).
Start the cooking process.
When the vegetables and pork are cooked, put them in the blending bowl and set aside the cooking liquid.
Blend, adding the olive oil and some of the cooking liquid to bring to the desired consistency. Add a little hot water if there is not enough cooking liquid.
If desired, add the cinnamon and blend again.
Serve immediately. You may also store in Béaba storage containers refrigerated up to 3 days or freeze.

Foodie Fact

Sweet potato and apple combined creates a smooth texture and provides plenty of gentle fiber to aid in baby's digestion of the pork.

8+ MONTHS

Moroccan-Style Chicken

PREP TIME
5 min

COOK TIME
15 min

WATER
Level 3

Ingredients:

1 ½ cup cubed carrots
½ cup cubed potato
1 ounce cubed chicken breast
1 teaspoon olive oil
Pinch of cumin (optional)

Foodie Fact

Add a pinch of cumin to aid in digestion and begin introducing spices to baby's palette.

Steps:

Put the carrots, potato, and chicken in the steamer basket.
Pour water into the tank (level 3).
Start the cooking process.
When the vegetables and chicken are cooked, put them in the blending bowl and set aside the cooking liquid.
Blend, adding the olive oil and some of the cooking liquid to bring to the desired consistency.
If desired, add the cumin and blend again.
Serve immediately. You may also store in Béaba storage containers refrigerated up to 3 days or freeze.

8+ MONTHS

Steak and Taters

PREP TIME
5 min

COOK TIME
15 min

WATER
Level 3

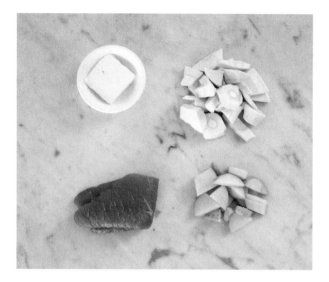

Ingredients:

1 ½ cups cubed parsnips
½ cup cubed potato
1 ounce cubed lean steak
1 pat of butter

Steps:

Put the parsnips, potato, and steak in the steamer basket.
Pour water into the tank (level 3).
Start the cooking process.
When the vegetables and steak are cooked, put them in the blending bowl and set aside the cooking liquid.
Blend, adding the butter and some of the cooking liquid to bring to the desired consistency.
Serve immediately. You may also store in Béaba storage containers refrigerated up to 3 days or freeze.

Foodie Fact

Parsnips have a sweet and nutty flavor that baby will love. They're a great alternative to carrots and provide a bit of fiber and protein.

8+ MONTHS

Salmon and Potato Purée

PREP TIME
5 min

COOK TIME
15 min

WATER
Level 3

Ingredients:

1 ½ cups cubed sweet potato
½ cup cubed potato
1 ounce de-boned and cubed salmon
Pinch of dill
1 teaspoon olive oil

Steps:

Put the potatoes and salmon in the steamer basket
and sprinkle dill over top.
Pour into the tank (level 3).
Start the cooking process.
When the potatoes and salmon are cooked, put them
in the blending bowl and set aside the cooking liquid.
Blend, adding the olive oil and some of the cooking
liquid to bring to the desired consistency.
*Serve immediately. You may also store in Béaba
storage containers refrigerated up to 3 days or freeze.*

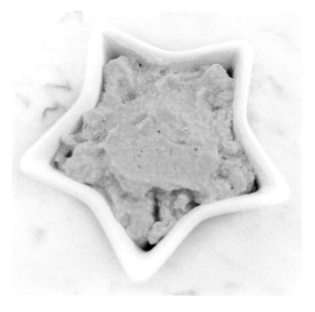

Foodie Fact

*Add a pinch of dill to for extra vitamins A and C.
It will also aid in baby's digestion and help reduce
gas from other foods.*

8+ MONTHS

Porky's Purée

PREP TIME	COOK TIME	WATER
5 min	15 min	Level 3

Ingredients:

1 ½ cups thinly sliced carrots
½ cup cooked rice
1 ounce cubed rindless
cooked ham
1 teaspoon olive oil

Steps:

Put the carrots in the steamer basket.
Pour water into the tank (level 3).
Start the cooking process.
When the carrots are cooked, put them, the cooked rice, and ham in the blending bowl and set aside the cooking liquid.
Blend, adding the olive oil and some of the cooking liquid to bring to the desired consistency.
Serve immediately. You may also store in Béaba storage containers refrigerated up to 3 days or freeze.

Foodie Fact

Ham is a great protein alternative to chicken. For the healthiest option, be sure to buy organic and nitrate-free meats.

8+ MONTHS

Steak Dinner

PREP TIME
5 min

COOK TIME
15 min

WATER
Level 3

Ingredients:

1 ½ cups cubed turnips
½ cup diced green beans
1 ounce cubed lean steak
½ cup cooked quinoa
1 pat of butter

Foodie Fact
Quinoa is high in protein and contains essential amino acids necessary for baby's healthy growth.

Steps:

Put the turnips, green beans, and steak in the steamer basket.
Pour water into the tank (level 3).
Start the cooking process.
When the vegetables and steak are cooked, put them and the cooked quinoa into the blending bowl and set aside the cooking liquid.
Blend, adding the butter and some of the cooking liquid to bring to the desired consistency.
Serve immediately. You may also store in Béaba storage containers refrigerated up to 3 days or freeze.

8+ MONTHS

Tuna
Casserole

PREP TIME
5 min

COOK TIME
15 min

WATER
Level 3

Ingredients:

1 ½ cup chopped broccoli florets
1 ounce canned tuna fish in oil
½ cup cooked couscous
1 teaspoon olive oil

Steps:

Put the broccoli in the steamer basket.
Pour water into the tank (level 3).
Start the cooking process.
When cooking is completed, put the broccoli instead
of, the cooked couscous, and the tuna fish in the
blending bowl and set aside the cooking liquid.
Blend, adding the olive oil and some of the cooking
liquid to bring to the desired consistency.
*Serve immediately. You may also store in Béaba
storage containers refrigerated up to 3 days or freeze.*

🔍 *Foodie Fact*
*Tuna is a great source of Omega 3 fats, which are
essential for baby's brain and eye development.*

8+ MONTHS

Swiss Zucchini Purée

 PREP TIME
5 min

COOK TIME
15 min

WATER
Level 3

Ingredients:

1 cup cubed zucchini
½ cup cubed potato
¾ ounce of creamy Swiss cheese

Steps:

Put the zucchini and potatoes in the steamer basket.
Pour water into the tank (level 3).
Start the cooking process.
Once the vegetables are cooked, put them and the cheese in the blending bowl and set aside the cooking liquid.
Blend, adding some of the cooking liquid to bring to the desired consistency. Add a little hot water if there is not enough cooking liquid.
Serve immediately. You may also store in Béaba storage containers refrigerated up to 3 days or freeze.

Foodie Fact

Cheese is loaded with calcium, protein and vitamins A and D, which are important for baby's muscle, tissue, and organ development.

8+ MONTHS

Sunshine Cream of Chicken

PREP TIME
5 min

COOK TIME
15 min

WATER
Level 3

Ingredients:

½ cup cubed sweet potato
¼ cup cubed carrots
½ cup cubed apples
2 ounces cubed chicken breast
¼ cup sliced ripe banana
Milk or coconut milk, to taste
(optional)

🔍 Foodie Fact
For children 12 months and older, add coconut milk to support brain health and boost immunity.

Steps:

Put the sweet potato, carrots, apple, and chicken breast in the steamer basket.
Pour water into the tank (level 3).
Start the cooking process.
When the vegetables and chicken are cooked, put them in the blending bowl with the banana and set aside the cooking liquid.
Blend, adding some of the cooking liquid to bring to the desired consistency.
Serve immediately. You may also store in Béaba storage containers refrigerated up to 3 days or freeze.

8+ MONTHS

Carrot, Apple, and Potato Soup

PREP TIME
5 min

COOK TIME
15 min

WATER
Level 3

Ingredients:

½ cup cubed potato
½ cup cubed sweet potato
¼ cup sliced carrots

½ cup cubed apple
Pinch of salt (optional)
Pinch of cinnamon
(optional)

Steps:

Put the potato, sweet potato, carrots, and apple in the steamer basket.
Pour water into the tank (level 3).
Start the cooking process.
When the vegetables are cooked, place them in the blending bowl and set aside the cooking liquid.
Blend, adding some of the cooking liquid to bring to the desired consistency.
You may thin by adding warm water.
If desired, add a pinch of sea salt (for children at least 12 months old) and cinnamon to the mixture and blend.
Serve immediately. You may also store in Béaba storage containers refrigerated up to 3 days or freeze.

Foodie Fact
This sweet and savory soup is loaded with gentle fiber, calcium, and vitamin K.

Mini Mama's Meatballs

PREP TIME	10 min
COOK TIME	25 min
WATER	Level 1

Ingredients

1 tablespoon cubed onion
¼ cup sliced carrot
¼ cup cubed zucchini
¼ cup sliced mushrooms
1 teaspoon fresh thyme
1 egg white
1 tablespoon olive oil
1 tablespoon tomato paste or ketchup
1 teaspoon oregano

¼ cup breadcrumbs
Pinch of salt and pepper (optional)
Pinch of garlic powder (optional)
1 tablespoon Parmesan cheese (optional)
6 ounces ground beef or ground turkey breast

Serve with:
1 recipe Plum Tomato Sauce, heated

Steps:

Preheat the oven to 375° F.
Put the onion, carrot, zucchini, mushrooms, and thyme in the steamer basket.
Pour water into the tank (level 1).
Start the cooking process.
When the vegetables are cooked, remove them from the steamer basket and place in a bowl to cool. Discard cooking liquid.
When vegetables are cool enough to handle, put them in the blending bowl along with the egg white, olive oil, tomato paste, oregano, and breadcrumbs and blend. For children 12 months or older, also add salt, pepper, garlic powder, Parmesan cheese.
Add beef or turkey to bowl and pulse to mix. Don't overwork.
Remove to a large bowl.
Measure out about a tablespoon of meat and gently roll the meatballs in the palm of your hand to shape.
Place the meatballs on a parchment-lined pan or in a non-stick mini muffin pan.
Bake for 20 to 25 minutes or until the internal temperature of the meatballs reaches 165° F.
Toss with Plum Tomato Sauce *(page 53)*.
You may also brown the meatballs in a non-stick sauté pan with 2 tablespoons of olive oil until crispy on all sides. Drain on a sheet pan lined with paper towel. Continue with baking instructions.
Serve immediately. You may also store in Béaba storage containers refrigerated up to 3 days or freeze.

8+ MONTHS

Apple Sauce

🥣 PREP TIME
5 min

⏱ COOK TIME
15 min

💧 WATER
Level 3

Ingredients:

2 - 3 cups cubed apples, or whatever quantity fills the steamer basket.
1 pinch of cinnamon (optional)

Steps:

Put the apples in the steamer basket.
Pour water into the tank (level 3).
Start the cooking process.
When the apples are cooked, put them in the blending bowl and set aside the cooking liquid.
Blend, adding some of the cooking liquid to bring to the desired consistency.
If desired, add the cinnamon and blend again.
Serve immediately. You may also store in Béaba storage containers refrigerated up to 3 days or freeze.

🔍 *Foodie Fact*
Introduce a new spice to baby by adding a pinch of cinnamon for an antioxidant boost and to help regulate baby's blood sugar.

8+ MONTHS

Apple Raisin Compote

PREP TIME
5 min

COOK TIME
15 min

WATER
Level 2

Ingredients:

½ cup cubed apple
1 date, pitted
10 raisins

Steps:

Put the apple, date, and raisins in the steamer basket.
Pour water into the tank (level 2).
Start the cooking process.
When the fruits are cooked, place them in the blending bowl and set aside some of the cooking liquid.
Blend, adding some of the cooking liquid to bring to the desired consistency
Serve immediately.

Q *Foodie Fact*
Raisins are loaded with fiber, vitamins and minerals. This compote is a healthy option for topping oatmeal, pancakes, or toast.

Growing Baby:

Meal ideas for a growing appetite

12+	MONTHS

BÉABA

BABYCOOK BOOK

12+ MONTHS

Curried Carrot Ginger Soup

PREP TIME
10 min

COOK TIME
15 min

WATER
Level 3

Ingredients

1 tablespoon cubed onion
1 cup cubed carrots
¾ cup cubed sweet potato
½ teaspoon fresh grated ginger
½ teaspoon fresh grated turmeric
(or ¼ teaspoon ground turmeric powder)

½ cup chicken broth
Pinch garlic powder or ½ a garlic clove
½ teaspoon sweet curry powder
Pinch of salt and pepper
½ cup coconut milk (full fat)

Steps:

Put the onion, carrots, and sweet potato in the steamer basket with ginger and turmeric.
Pour water into the tank (level 3).
Start the cooking process.
When the vegetables are cooked, put them in the blending bowl and set aside the cooking liquid.
Add chicken broth, garlic, curry powder, salt and pepper, and coconut milk and blend to a purée.
If needed, blend, adding some of the cooking liquid to bring to the desired consistency.
Serve immediately. You may also store in Béaba storage containers up to 4 days or freeze.

🔍 *Foodie Fact*
Turmeric has excellent anti-inflammatory benefits, helps fight infection and reduces blood sugar. Add it to soups and savory dishes to give baby a healthy boost.

12+ MONTHS

Chicken Ratatouille

PREP TIME	COOK TIME	WATER
10 min	25 min	Level 2 & 3

Ingredients

¼ cup cubed zucchini
¼ cup cubed summer squash
¼ cup cubed red onion
¼ cup cubed red bell pepper
¼ cup cubed eggplant

2 ounces cubed chicken breast
1 teaspoon tomato paste
1 basil leaf, chopped
½ teaspoon chopped fresh thyme
Pinch of salt

Pinch of garlic powder
1 teaspoon olive oil
¼ cup cooked quinoa
Serve with:
½ cup Plum Tomato Sauce

Steps:

Put the zucchini, summer squash, red onion, red pepper, and eggplant in the steamer basket.
Pour water into the tank (level 2).
Start the cooking process.
When the vegetables are cooked, remove them to a bowl.
Rub chicken cubes with tomato paste, basil, thyme, salt, and garlic powder.
Put the chicken in steamer basket.
Pour water into the tank (level 3).
Start the cooking process.
When the chicken is cooked, add it to the bowl with vegetables, olive oil, and cooked quinoa and toss with warmed *Plum Tomato Sauce (page 53)*.
Serve immediately. You may also store in Béaba storage containers refrigerated up to 4 days or freeze.

🔍 *Foodie Fact*

Chicken and quinoa combined make this a high protein dish. The bell pepper adds an extra layer of flavor to help continue building baby's palette.

12+ MONTHS

Chicken Parm Bites

 PREP TIME
10 min

 COOK TIME
20 min

WATER
None

Ingredients:

1/3 cup grated Mozzarella
cheese
¼ cup breadcrumbs
Pinch of garlic powder
Pinch of Italian seasoning
Pinch of salt
4 ounces cubed chicken breast
1 egg, beaten

For breading:
1 cup breadcrumbs, plus 2
tablespoons grated Parmesan
cheese

Serve with:
1 cup *Plum Tomato Sauce*
(page 53)

Steps:

Preheat oven to 350° F.
Put Mozzarella cheese, breadcrumbs, garlic powder, Italian seasoning, and
salt in the blending bowl and pulse to combine. Remove to a bowl.
Put the chicken in the blending bowl and pulse to break down.
Remove chicken to bowl with cheese, breadcrumbs, and seasonings.
Gently fold together just until mixed. Don't overwork.
Use a tablespoon to scoop chicken mix onto a baking sheet lined with
parchment paper. Gently flatten the dollops with your hands.
Dip each flattened chicken patty into the egg and then gently coat with
breadcrumb / Parmesan mix and return to baking sheet.
Bake for about 20 minutes or until internal temperature reaches 165° F.
Serve immediately with warmed Plum Tomato Sauce to dip. You may also
refrigerate in Béaba storage containers for up to 4 days or freeze.

Foodie Fact

Mixing Mozzarella into the
breading adds a boost of calcium
and vitamins A and D. Plus, baby
will love the cheesy taste.

12+ MONTHS

Plum Tomato Sauce

PREP TIME
5 min

COOK TIME
15 min

WATER
Level 3

Ingredients:

1 cup seeded, chopped plum tomatoes
2 to 3 fresh basil leaves
1 teaspoon olive oil
1 tablespoon tomato paste
Pinch of garlic powder or ½ clove of garlic (optional)
Pinch of salt (optional)
1 tablespoon grated Parmesan cheese (optional)

Steps:

Put the tomatoes in steamer basket.
Pour water into the tank (level 3).
Start the cooking process.
When tomatoes are cooked, put them, and the basil, olive oil, and tomato paste in the blending bowl, and blend to desired consistency.
If desired, add the garlic, salt, and Parmesan cheese (for children at least 12 months old) and blend again. You may also simmer sauce on the stovetop for 10 minutes longer to further cook the tomatoes.
Serve immediately over pasta or Mini Mama's Meatballs (page 42). You may also store in Béaba storage containers refrigerated up to 3 days or freeze.

Foodie Fact
Tomatoes are heart-healthy and offer an abundance of vitamins A, C and K.

12+ MONTHS

Chicken, Broccoli and Cheddar Tots

PREP TIME	COOK TIME	WATER
15 min	25 min	Level 2

Ingredients

1 cup golden cracker crumbs, (use crackers like Ritz)
1 cup chopped broccoli florets
4 ounces cubed chicken breast

1/3 cup grated Cheddar cheese
Pinch of Old Bay Seasoning
(or salt and pepper)

Steps:

Preheat oven to 375° F. Put the crackers in blending bowl and pulse to fine crumb. Remove to a bowl.
Put the broccoli in the steamer basket.
Pour water into the tank (level 2).
Start the cooking process.
Remove the broccoli to its own bowl to cool. Discard cooking liquid.
Put the chicken in blending bowl and pulse to break down.
Remove chicken to bowl with broccoli. Add cheddar cheese and Old Bay Seasoning. Gently fold together just until mixed. Don't overwork.
Use a tablespoon to scoop chicken mix onto a baking sheet lined with parchment paper. Form into tots with your hands.
Roll each tot in cracker crumbs to coat lightly and place back on baking sheet.
Bake in 375° F oven 20 to 25 minutes or until internal temperature reaches 165° F.
Serve immediately, alone or with ketchup. You may also store in Béaba storage container refrigerated up to 4 days or freeze.

🔍 *Foodie Fact*
Kids love this yummy, healthy finger food. These tots are great for sneaking more vitamin-rich broccoli onto the menu.

12+ MONTHS

Autumn Steak

PREP TIME
5 min

COOK TIME
15 min

WATER
Level 3

Ingredients

¼ cup chopped cauliflower florets
¼ cup cubed potato
1 tablespoon cubed onion

1 ½ ounces chopped lean steak
1 teaspoon olive oil
¼ teaspoon thyme

Steps:

Put the cauliflower, potato, onion and steak in the steamer basket.
Pour water into the tank (level 3).
Start the cooking process.
When the steak and vegetables are cooked, put them in the blending bowl and set aside some of the cooking liquid.
Blend, adding the olive oil and some of the cooking liquid to bring to the desired consistency.
Add the thyme and blend again.
Serve immediately. You may also store in Béaba storage containers refrigerated up to 3 days.containers refrigerated for up to 3 days or freeze.

🔍 *Foodie Fact*
For the healthiest red meat, buy organic, hormone-free, grass-fed beef.

12+ MONTHS

Meatloaf Muffins with Potato Icing

PREP TIME
20 min

COOK TIME
30 min

WATER
Level 3

Ingredients

1 recipe Mini Mama's
Meatballs mix *(page 42)*,
uncooked

1 cup cubed potato
1 tablespoon butter
Pinch of salt

Steps:

Preheat oven to 375° F.
Put the potatoes in the steamer basket.
Pour water into the tank (level 3).
Start the cooking process.
When the potatoes are cooked, put them in the blending bowl.
Add butter, blend to the desired consistency.
Scoop Mini Mama's Meatball mix into Béaba Multiportions Silicone tray.
Top with about 1 tablespoon of mashed potato and spread over surface of each muffin.
Bake in oven for 25 to 30 minutes or until internal temperature of meatloaf muffins reaches 165° F.
Remove from container to serve. You may also store in Béaba Multiportions Silicone tray refrigerated for up to 3 days or freeze.

🔍 *Foodie Fact* ─────────

This dish is filled with vitamins and healthy carbohydrates. The muffin-like presentation makes mealtime more fun for kids.

12+ MONTHS

Rosemary Mushroom Purée

PREP TIME	COOK TIME	WATER
15 min	25 min	Level 2

Ingredients:

1 ½ cups sliced mushrooms, button or assorted
¼ cup cubed golden potato
1 teaspoon chopped fresh thyme

1 teaspoon chopped fresh rosemary
1 tablespoon grated Fontina cheese

1 tablespoon butter or olive oil
1 to 2 tablespoons of milk or cream
Pinch of garlic powder
Pinch of salt and pepper to taste

Steps:

Put the mushrooms and potato in the steamer basket.
Top with chopped fresh thyme and rosemary.
Pour water into the tank (level 2).
Start the cooking process.
When the vegetables are cooked, put them in the blending bowl.
Add the grated Fontina cheese, butter or oil, and 1 to 2 tablespoons of milk or cream.
Blend to bring to the desired consistency.
Add garlic powder, salt and pepper to taste and blend again.
Serve immediately. You may also store in Béaba storage containers refrigerated for up to 3 days or freeze.

Q Foodie Fact
Mushrooms are a hearty, flavorful alternative to meat and provide baby a good supply of vitamin D, iron, and antioxidants.

12+ MONTHS

Salmon and Greens

PREP TIME
5 min

COOK TIME
15 min

WATER
Level 3

Ingredients:

¼ cup cubed potatoes
1 ounce de-boned and cubed salmon
1 cup frozen spinach
1 pat of butter

Steps:

Put the potatoes, salmon, and spinach in the steamer basket.
Pour the water into the water tank (level 3).
Start the cooking process.
When the salmon and vegetables are cooked, put them in the blending bowl and set aside the cooking liquid.
Blend, adding the butter and some of the cooking liquid to bring to the desired consistency.
Serve immediately. You may also store in Béaba storage containers refrigerated for up to 3 days or freeze.

Foodie Fact —————

Add a fresh squeeze of lemon to optimize the amount of iron baby can absorb from the spinach.

12+ MONTHS

Winter Squash and Ham

| PREP TIME 5 min | COOK TIME 15 min | WATER Level 3 |

Ingredients:

- 2 cup cubed butternut or acorn squash
- 2 dried apricots
- 2 ounce cubed cooked ham
- ½ cup cooked couscous
- 1 pat of butter

🔍 *Foodie Fact*

Baby will love the sweet taste of dried apricots, which are full of iron and vitamins A and C.

Steps:

Put the squash and apricots in the steamer basket.
Pour the water into the water tank (level 3).
Start the cooking process.
When the squash mix is cooked, put it in the blending bowl and set aside the cooking liquid.
Add the cooked ham, cooked couscous, and butter.
Blend, adding some of the cooking liquid to bring to the desired consistency.
Serve immediately. You may also store in Béaba storage containers refrigerated for up to 3 days or freeze.

12+ MONTHS

Spanish-Style Chicken

PREP TIME
5 min

COOK TIME
15 min

WATER
Level 3

Ingredients

1 cup chopped tomatoes
½ cup thinly sliced red bell peppers

2 ounces cubed chicken breast
½ cup cooked rice
1 teaspoon olive oil

Steps:

Put the tomatoes, red peppers, and chicken in the steamer basket.
Pour the water into the water tank (level 3).
Start the cooking process.
When the vegetables and chicken are cooked, put them in the blending bowl along with the cooked rice and set aside the cooking liquid.
Blend, adding the olive oil and some of the cooking liquid to bring to the desired consistency.
Serve immediately. You may also store in Béaba storage containers refrigerated for up to 3 days or freeze.

Foodie Fact

For a healthier choice, use brown rice, which is loaded with B-Complex, fiber, and essential fatty acids.

Peppery Pork and Taters

PREP TIME
5 min

COOK TIME
15 min

WATER
Level 3

Ingredients:

¼ cup cubed red bell peppers
¼ cup cubed onions
¼ cup cubed potatoes
1 ounce cubed pork tenderloin
1 teaspoon olive oil

Foodie Fact

Bell peppers are a great source of vitamins C and E and potassium. In this dish, they help baby get used to new textures and flavors.

Steps:

Put the red peppers, onions, potatoes, and pork tenderloin in the steamer basket.
Pour the water into the water tank (level 3).
Start the cooking process.
When the vegetables and pork are cooked, put them in the blending bowl and set aside the cooking liquid.
Blend, adding the olive oil and some of the cooking liquid to bring to the desired consistency.
Serve immediately. You may also store in Béaba storage containers refrigerated for up to 3 days or freeze.

12+ MONTHS

Martian Purée

⌣ PREP TIME
5 min

⏱ COOK TIME
15 min

💧 WATER
Level 3

Ingredients:

1 ½ cup chopped broccoli florets
2 ounce ground beef
½ cup cooked polenta
2 tablespoons grated Mozzarella cheese
1 teaspoon olive oil

Steps:

Put the broccoli and ground beef in the steamer basket.
Pour water into the tank (level 3).
Start the cooking process.
When the beef mixture is cooked, place it in the blending bowl and set aside some of the cooking liquid. Add the cooked polenta, mozzarella cheese, and olive oil. Blend, adding some of the cooking liquid to bring to the desired consistency.
Serve immediately. You may also store in Béaba storage containers refrigerated for up to 3 days or freeze.

🔍 *Foodie Fact*

Soft polenta is a great alternative to rice and provides a smoother, creamier texture that baby will love. This dish is loaded with hidden broccoli to give baby a vitamin boost.

12+ MONTHS

Creamy Butternut Sauce

PREP TIME
5 min

COOK TIME
15 min

WATER
Level 3

Ingredients:

1 cup cubed butternut squash
1 tablespoon heavy cream
1 tablespoon butter
Pinch of cinnamon or nutmeg
(optional)
Pinch of salt and pepper (optional)

Foodie Fact
Sneak in an extra serving of
vegetables by pouring this sauce
over broccoli for a healthier take
on "broccoli and cheese".

Steps:

Put the squash in the steamer basket.
Pour water into the tank (level 3).
Start the cooking process.
When the squash is cooked, place it in the blending bowl with the heavy cream and butter and set aside the cooking liquid.
Blend, adding some of the cooking liquid to bring to the desired consistency.
If desired, add the cinnamon or nutmeg and pinch of salt and pepper and blend again.
Serve immediately over pasta or vegetables. You may also store in Béaba storage containers refrigerated up to 3 days or freeze.

12+ MONTHS

Canadian Crumble

🍶 PREP TIME
5 min

⏱ COOK TIME
10 min

💧 WATER
Level 2

Ingredients:

1 cup cubed apple
1 vanilla wafer, crumbled
1 teaspoon maple syrup

Steps:

Place the apples in the steamer basket.
Pour water into the tank (level 2).
Start the cooking process.
Mix the crumbled vanilla wafer with maple syrup.
When the apples are cooked, place the cooked apple in a small dish and cover with the vanilla wafer/maple syrup mixture.
Serve immediately.

🔍 *Foodie Fact*
Pure maple syrup is loaded with beneficial minerals and contains no artificial colors or corn syrup. Use it as a sugar substitute for a healthy dose of sweetness.

12+ MONTHS

Yogurt and Vanilla Pear

PREP TIME
5 min

COOK TIME
10 min

WATER
Level 2

Ingredients:

Steps:

1 cup cubed pear
½ teaspoon vanilla extract
1 cup plain whole milk Greek yogurt

Q *Foodie Fact* ————

*Greek yogurt is rich in protein
and probiotics, which will keep
baby feeling full while promoting
a healthy tummy.*

Put the pear in the steamer basket.
Pour water into the tank (level 2).
Start the cooking process.
When cooking is completed, put the pear and the yogurt in the blending
bowl and blend.
Add the vanilla extract and blend again.
*Serve immediately. You may also store in Béaba storage containers
refrigerated for up to 3 days.*

12+ MONTHS

Berry Parfait

	PREP TIME
	5 min

	COOK TIME
	10 min

	WATER
	Level 2

Ingredients:

½ cup raspberries
½ cup blueberries
1 cup plain whole milk Greek yogurt

Steps:

Put the raspberries and blueberries in the steamer basket.
Pour water into the tank (level 2).
Start the cooking process.
When the fruit is cooked, put it in the blending bowl and discard the cooking liquid.
Blend, adding a little water if necessary to bring to the desired consistency.
Arrange in a small glass, alternating layers of blended fruit and layers of yogurt.
Serve immediately. You may also store in Béaba storage containers refrigerated for up to 3 days or freeze.

🔍 *Foodie Fact*

Berries are a great source of vitamins and anti-oxidants, making this recipe a great breakfast for the whole family!

12+ MONTHS

Little Red Soup

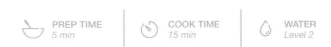

PREP TIME
5 min

COOK TIME
15 min

WATER
Level 2

Ingredients:

2 cups cubed strawberries
6 mint leaves

Foodie Fact

Mint is great for soothing baby's tummy aches and fighting off unhealthy bacteria.

Steps:

Put the strawberries in the steamer basket.
Pour water into the tank (level 2).
Start the cooking process.
When the fruit is cooked, put it and the mint leaves in the blending bowl.
Blend, adding a small amount of water to bring to the desired consistency.
Serve immediately. You may also store in Béaba storage containers refrigerated for up to 3 days or freeze.

Little Tikes:

Tasty toddler meals

18+	MONTHS

BABYCOOK® BOOK

18+ MONTHS

Cod Cakes

PREP TIME	COOK TIME	WATER
10 min	45 min	Level 3

Ingredients

1 cup golden cracker crumbs
(use crackers like Ritz)
½ cup cubed potato
3 ounces cod fillet, cubed
1 teaspoon chopped fresh dill
1 teaspoon chopped fresh
parsley
¼ cup finely chopped celery
Pinch of garlic powder
Pinch of Old Bay Seasoning (or
salt and pepper)
Squeeze of fresh lemon
1 tablespoon egg white
1 tablespoon olive oil
1 tablespoon butter

Steps:

Put crackers in blending bowl and pulse to fine crumb. Remove to a bowl.
Put potatoes and cod in the steamer basket.
Pour water into the tank (level 3).
Start the cooking process.
When the potatoes and cod are cooked, put them in the blending bowl.
Discard cooking liquid.
Add dill and parsley and gently pulse 2 to 3 times. Remove to bowl.
Toss the mixture with celery, garlic powder, Old Bay Seasoning, squeeze of lemon, and egg white. Chill in the refrigerator for 15 to 30 minutes.
Form into small cakes and gently press in cracker crumbs to coat each side.
Heat the butter and olive oil a non-stick sauté pan over medium heat and pan-fry the cod cakes about 1 minute each side until golden brown.
Serve immediately. You may also store in Béaba storage containers refrigerated up to 3 days.

Foodie Fact

Cod fish is a great source of lean protein for kids. It has a mild taste and blends well with other foods.

18+ MONTHS

Potato Gratin

PREP TIME
10 min

COOK TIME
30 min

WATER
Level 3

Ingredients:

1 cup cubed potato
¼ cup cubed white onion
1 tablespoon cream cheese
1 tablespoon grated Swiss cheese

Steps:

Preheat the oven to 350° F
Put the potatoes in the steamer basket.
Pour water into the tank (level 3).
Start the cooking process.
When the potatoes are cooked, put them in the blending bowl and blend in the onion and cream cheese.
Scoop mixture into Béaba Multiportions Silicone tray.
Sprinkle the grated cheese on top.
Put in the oven for 15 minutes.
Let them cool before serving. You may also store in Béaba storage containers refrigerated up to 3 days.

Foodie Fact

This rich and creamy dish is full of calcium and kids love the yummy cheesy flavor.

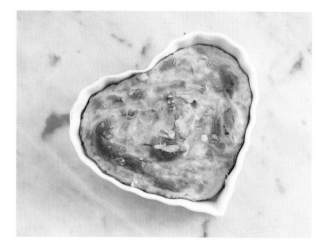

18+ MONTHS

Belgian Chicken

PREP TIME
10 min

COOK TIME
15 min

WATER
Level 3

Ingredients:

½ cup chopped brussels sprouts
1 ounce cubed chicken breast
¼ cup cubed potato
1 tablespoon grated Cheddar cheese

🔍 *Foodie Fact*

Brussels sprouts are full of vitamins C and K and are easily hidden in this delicious dish.

Steps:

Remove the outer leaves of the brussels sprouts, and finely chop the rest.
Put the chicken, brussels sprouts, and potato in the steamer basket.
Pour water into the tank (level 3).
Start the cooking process.
When the chicken and vegetables are cooked, put them in the blending bowl and set aside some of the cooking liquid.
Blend, adding some of the cooking liquid to bring to the desired consistency.
Add the cheddar and blend again.
Serve immediately. You may also store in Beaba storage containers refrigerated up to 3 days.

18+ MONTHS

Thai Pork

| | PREP TIME 5 min | COOK TIME 15 min | WATER Level 3 |

Ingredients:

¾ cup sliced carrots
1½ ounces pork tenderloin, cubed
¼ cup cooked rice
1 tablespoon coconut milk
Pinch of cumin

Foodie Fact

Coconut milk is an excellent dairy-free alternative that makes this dish rich and creamy.

Steps:

Put the carrots and pork in the steamer basket.
Pour water into the tank (level 3).
Start the cooking process.
When the carrots and pork are cooked, put them and the cooked rice in the blending bowl and set aside some of the cooking liquid.
Blend, adding the coconut milk and some of the cooking liquid to bring to the desired consistency.
Add the cumin and blend again.
Serve immediately. You may also store in Béaba storage containers refrigerated up to 3 days.

18+ MONTHS

Tuscan White Bean Soup

 PREP TIME
10 min

 COOK TIME
15 min

WATER
Level 3

Ingredients:

1 cup white beans, drained and rinsed
¼ cup cubed carrots
¼ cup cubed onion
1 tablespoon cooked bacon, chopped
1 tablespoon heavy cream
1 tablespoon olive oil
Pinch garlic powder or half a garlic clove
1 fresh sage leaf, chopped
Pinch of salt and pepper
1 tablespoon Parmesan cheese (optional)
½ teaspoon truffle oil (optional)

Steps:

Put white beans, carrots, and onion in the steamer basket.
Pour water into the tank (level 3).
Start the cooking process.
When the beans and vegetables are cooked, put them in the blending bowl and set aside the cooking liquid.
Add the bacon, cream, olive oil, garlic, sage, salt and pepper.
Blend, adding some of the cooking liquid to bring to the desired consistency.
Serve immediately. You may also store on Béaba storage containers refrigerated for up to 4 days.

For adults or babies 12+ months: Top soup with a pinch of Parmesan cheese and a drizzle of truffle oil.

🔍 *Foodie Fact* ————

Beans are rich in fiber, protein and carbohydrates making them a great energy source while helping regulate baby's blood sugar.

18+ MONTHS

Cauliflower Surprise

PREP TIME
5 min

COOK TIME
10 min

WATER
Level 2

Ingredients:

2 cups chopped cauliflower
florets
¼ cup cubed carrots
¼ cup peas (fresh or frozen)
¼ cup asparagus, tips only

Steps:

Put the cauliflower, carrots, and peas in the steamer basket.
Pour water into the tank (level 2).
Start the cooking process.
When the vegetables are are cooked, remove from steamer basket.
Discard cooking liquid.
Cool vegetable mixture.
Put the cooked vegetables in the blending bowl and pulse just until the vegetables are in rice-size pieces. Do not puree.
Serve immediately. You may also store in Béaba storage containers refrigerated up to 3 days.

For children 12 months and older or prenatal women, slice asparagus tops into small pieces and steam with cauliflower. Continue with instructions.

Foodie Fact

Cauliflower is an excellent source of vitamins B6, C, K and folate. The texture of this dish is similar to couscous and provides an opportunity to introduce something new to baby's developing palette.

18+ MONTHS

Pea Pancakes

PREP TIME
5 min

COOK TIME
20 min

WATER
Level 1

Ingredients

1 ½ cups green peas
(frozen or fresh)
1 egg
Pinch of salt

¼ cup flour
1 tablespoon olive oil
1 tablespoon butter for
serving

Steps:

Put the peas in the steamer basket.
Pour water into the tank (level 1).
Start the cooking process.
When the peas are cooked, cool to room temperature before proceeding. Discard cooking liquid.
Put the peas in the blending bowl, and add egg, salt and 2 tablespoons of water and blend until smooth. add flour and blend until just mixed in.
Heat 1 tablespoon of oïl in a non-stick skillet over medium heat, so oïl just coats the bottom of the pan.
Spoon batter into skillet in small 2-inch pancakes.
Cook gently about 2 to 3 minutes per side (batter will form some bubbles).
Remove to a paper-towel lined plate and serve spread with butter.
Pancakes will keep refrigerated up to 4 days.

Note: If you want to keep the pancakes green, be careful not to brown at a higher heat.

Foodie Fact

These savory pea pancakes, filled with protein and fiber, make an excellent snack or fun side dish.

18+ MONTHS

Beet and Sweet Potato Pancakes

PREP TIME
10 min

COOK TIME
30 min

WATER
Level 3

Ingredients

¼ cup cubed sweet potatoes
1/2 cup beets, cubed
1 egg
½ teaspoon cinnamon
Pinch of salt

¼ cup flour
1 tablespoon olive or coconut oil
1 tablespoon coconut sugar (or maple syrup, honey or brown sugar)
Maple syrup for serving

Steps:

Put the sweet potatoes and beet in the steamer basket.
Pour water into the tank (level 3).
Start the cooking process.
When vegetables are done cooking, allow them to cool to room temperature. Discard cooking liquid.
Put the vegetables in the blending bowl, and add egg, cinnamon, salt, and 1 tablespoon water and blend until smooth. Add flour and blend until just mixed in.
Heat 1 tablespoon oil in a non-stick skillet over medium heat, so oil just coats bottom of the pan.
Spoon batter into skillet in small 2-inch pancakes. Cook gently about 2 to 3 minutes per side (batter will form some bubbles).
Remove to a paper towel lined plate.
Serve with coconut sugar or another sweetener of your choice.
Pancakes will keep refrigerated up to 4 days.

Note: If you want to keep the pancakes pink, be careful not to brown at a higher heat.

Foodie Fact
Beets are fiber-filled and blend well into both sweet and savory dishes.

18+ MONTHS

Autumn Crumble

PREP TIME
5 min

COOK TIME
10 min

WATER
Level 2

Ingredients:

Steps:

¼ cup sliced banana
¼ cup cubed plums
¼ cup cubed apples
1 vanilla wafer, crumbled

Foodie Fact ───────
Bananas are rich in potassium and add a velvety texture to this dessert.

Put the banana, plums, and apples in the steamer basket.
Pour water into the tank (level 2).
Start the cooking process.
When the fruits are cooked, remove them to the blending bowl and set aside some of the cooking liquid.
Blend, adding some of the cooking liquid to bring to the desired consistency.
Put the mixture in a small dish and cover with the crumbled vanilla wafer.
Serve immediately.

18+ MONTHS

Apple
Glaze

PREP TIME
5 min

COOK TIME
10 min

WATER
Level 2

Ingredients:

1/3 cup cubed apple
1 tablespoon maple syrup

Steps:

Put the apple in the steamer basket.
Pour water into the tank (level 2).
Start the cooking process.
When the apple is cooked, put it in the blending bowl.
Discard cooking liquid.
Add maple syrup and blend to desired consistency.
Serve immediately.

18+ MONTHS

New England-Style Meatloaf Muffins with Apple Glaze

PREP TIME
10 min

COOK TIME
35 min

WATER
Level 1

Ingredients

½ cup diced apple
¼ cup diced celery
¼ cup diced onion
1 teaspoon fresh thyme
6 ounces chicken breast, cubed

1 egg white
1 teaspoon olive oil
¼ cup breadcrumbs
¼ cup dried cranberries

Steps:

Preheat oven to 375° F.
Put the apple, celery, onion, and thyme in the steamer basket.
Pour water into the tank (level 1).
Start the cooking process.
Once the vegetables are cooked, set them aside in a small bowl to cool. Discard cooking liquid.
Add cooked and cooled vegetables, egg white, olive oil, raw chicken and breadcrumbs to the blending bowl and blend. Don't overwork.
Remove the mixture to a large bowl and fold in cranberries.
Scoop meatloaf mix into the Béaba Multiportions Silicone tray. Top each muffin with 1 teaspoon of Apple Glaze.
Bake in oven for 25 to 30 minutes until internal temperature of meatloaf muffin reaches 165° F.
Remove from container to serve. You may also store in Béaba storage containers refrigerated up to 3 days or freeze.

Foodie Fact

This alternative to traditional meatloaf uses chicken for lean protein, and cranberries for an anti-oxidant boost.

18+ MONTHS

Sweet Red Compote

PREP TIME
5 min

COOK TIME
10 min

WATER
Level 2

Ingredients:

¾ cup cubed apples
1 cup red seedless grapes
¾ cup raspberries

🔍 *Foodie Fact*
This sweet treat has plenty of gentle fiber, which makes it the perfect dessert to aid in baby's digestion.

Steps:

Put the apples, grapes, and raspberries in the steamer basket.
Pour water into the tank (level 2).
Start the cooking process.
When the fruits are cooked, place them in the blending bowl and set aside the cooking liquid.
Blend, adding some of the cooking liquid to bring to the desired consistency.
Serve immediately. You may also store in Béaba storage containers refrigerated up to 3 days or freeze.

18+ MONTHS

Strawberry Apple Crumble

PREP TIME
5 min

COOK TIME
10 min

WATER
Level 2

Ingredients:

½ cup cubed apple
½ cup quartered strawberries
1 vanilla wafer, crumbled

Foodie Fact

Strawberries and apples combined provide plenty of vitamins and gentle fiber. This sweet treat is a great healthy dessert option.

Steps:

Put the apple in the steamer basket.
Pour water into the tank (level 2).
Start the cooking process.
When the apple is cooked, put it in the blending bowl and blend.
Add the strawberries and blend.
Put the strawberry and apple mixture in a small dish and cover with the crumbled vanilla wafer.
Serve immediately.

Beyond Baby:

Prenatal, postnatal and family recipes

FAMILY

BÉABA

BABYCOOK **BOOK**

FAMILY

Oven-Baked Carrot Fries with Yogurt Dill Dipping Sauce

 PREP TIME
10 min

COOK TIME
45 min

WATER
None

Ingredients:

Steps:

1 pound carrots, cut into matchsticks
2 tablespoons olive oil
1 teaspoon dried thyme or fresh chopped rosemary
1 tablespoon maple syrup, honey, or coconut sugar
Pinch of salt and pepper to taste

Preheat oven to 425° F. Line a baking sheet with parchment paper.
In a large blending bowl, toss the carrot sticks, olive oil, herbs, sugar, salt, and pepper. Toss well to coat.
Roast in the oven until carrots are well browned and tender, about 20 to 30 minutes. Remove from oven and cool on the sheet pan.
Serve immediately with Yogurt Dill Dipping Sauce (page 100).

Foodie Fact

A great alternative to regular fries, these healthy carrot fries are loaded with vitamin A and calcium.

FAMILY

Yogurt Dill Dipping Sauce

Ingredients:

1 cup plain Greek yogurt
¼ cup lemon juice (from about half a lemon)
1 tablespoon honey
Pinch of salt and pepper
¼ cup stemmed and chopped fresh dill

Steps:

Put all the ingredients in the blending bowl and blend until smooth.
Serve immediately. You may also store in Béaba storage containers refrigerated up to 3 days.

🔍 *Foodie Fact*
In addition to serving with Oven Baked Carrot Fries, this is also a great dip for raw veggies and crackers or pita bread.

FAMILY

Sweet Soy Dipping Sauce

Ingredients:

4 tablespoons soy sauce
4 tablespoons rice vinegar
4 tablespoons brown sugar or maple syrup
1 teaspoon sesame oil
2 tablespoon water
Pinch of fresh grated ginger (optional)
2 teaspoon minced scallion (optional)

Steps:

Put all the ingredients in the blending bowl and blend to combine.
Serve with Shrimp and Chicken Shumai Dumplings (page 102).

Foodie Fact
Sesame Oil contains natural anti-bacterial and anti-oxidant properties making this sauce super tasty and super healthy.

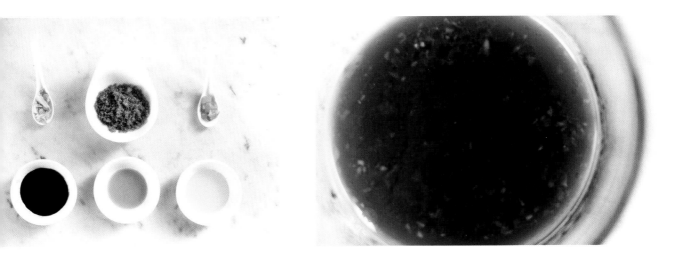

FAMILY

Shrimp and Chicken Shumai Dumplings

PREP TIME
25 min

COOK TIME
20 min

WATER
Level 1 & 3

Ingredients

¼ cup diced carrots
¼ cup sliced mushrooms
1 tablespoon chopped scallions
2 ounces chicken breast or pork, cubed
1 ounce shrimp, peeled, deveined, cubed
Pinch of salt
¼ teaspoon fresh grated ginger

¼ teaspoon sesame oil
½ teaspoon soy sauce
1 teaspoon cornstarch
2 large lettuce leaves
1 egg white
6 wonton wrappers

Steps:

Put the carrots, mushrooms, and scallions in the blending bowl and pulse to chop. Remove to small bowl.
Put the chicken and shrimp in the blending bowl with a pinch of salt and pulse to puree. Remove and wash the bowl. Chill filling up to 15 minutes.
Put the vegetable mix in the steamer basket. Pour water into the tank (level 1) and start the cooking process.
When the vegetables are cooked, remove from steamer basket. Discard the cooking liquid.
Put the cooked vegetables and chicken mix in the mixing bowl, add the grated ginger, sesame oil, soy sauce, and cornstarch. Pulse blend. Remove and wash the bowl.
Line steamer basket with one lettuce leaf.
Lay each wonton wrapper on a cutting board and brush with egg white.
Place 1 tablespoon of filling on each wonton wrapper; gather up the sides and pinch top to close.
Gently place 2 to 3 dumplings in the steamer basket, atop the lettuce leaf. Try to keep them from touching.
Pour water into the tank (level 3).
Start the cooking process.
When the dumplings are cooked, gently remove them from basket with a fork.
Repeat the process for the remaining dumplings.
Serve with Sweet Soy Dipping Sauce *(page 101)*.

FAMILY

Mini Egg Frittatas

PREP TIME
10 min

COOK TIME
15 min

WATER
None

Ingredients:

3 eggs
1 tablespoon heavy cream
¼ cup grated cheese
1 small pat of butter, softened
Pinch of salt and pepper
Up to 1 cup chopped vegetables
and/or meat (optional)

Steps:

Preheat oven to 375° F.
Crack eggs and pour in the blending bowl with cream, cheese, butter, and seasoning. Blend together.
Scoop into Béaba Multiportions Silicone tray.
Bake in oven for 12 to 15 minutes.
Do not overcook. Eggs are done when knife inserted comes out clean.
Cool in container and pop out to serve. You may also store in Béaba Multiportions Silicone tray refrigerated for up to 3 days.

Add-ins to make various Frittata variations:

Spinach and Feta
½ cup cooked spinach
¼ cup feta cheese

Put the feta and spinach in the blending bowl with egg mixture from frittata base recipe and blend until puréed.
Scoop into Béaba Multiportions Silicone tray and bake according to instructions.

Tomato and Broccoli
½ cup chopped, steamed broccoli
½ cup cubed tomato
¼ cup shredded Mozzarella cheese

Put the broccoli, tomato, and Mozzarella cheese in the blending bowl with the egg mixture from frittata base recipe and blend until puréed.
Scoop into Béaba Multiportions Silicone tray and bake according to instructions.

Western
½ cup diced, cooked bell peppers and onions
¼ cup cubed, cooked ham
¼ cup Swiss cheese, cubed

Put the peppers and onions, ham, and cheese in the blending bowl with the egg mixture from frittata base recipe and blend until puréed.
Scoop into Béaba Multiportions Silicone tray and bake according to instructions.

Cheddar and Chicken Sausage
½ cup cubed, cooked chicken sausage
¼ cup Cheddar cheese, shredded

Put the chicken sausage and Cheddar cheese in the blending bowl with the egg mixture from frittata base recipe and blend until puréed.
Scoop into Béaba Multiportions Silicone tray and bake according to instructions.

Foodie Fact

Eggs are a great source of protein, iron, and healthy cholesterol and help promote a well-developed immune system.

FAMILY

Super Greens Pesto

PREP TIME	COOK TIME	WATER
5 min	5min	None

Ingredients:

1 cup fresh baby spinach, packed
1 cup fresh baby kale, packed
3 to 4 basil leaves
½ cup almonds
1 tablespoon hemp seeds or pine nuts
¼ cup olive oil
Pinch of sea salt
Pinch of pepper
Squeeze of fresh lemon juice
Pinch of garlic powder (optional)
Grated Parmesan cheese (optional)

Steps:

Put all the ingredients in the blending bowl. Pulse until pesto starts to come together. Stop and scrape sides. Keep blending until desired pesto consistency is achieved.
Serve immediately over pasta or quinoa. You may also store in a store in a Béaba storage container refrigerated up to one week or freeze.

Foodie Fact

This highly nutrient-dense sauce is packed with super foods that help fight inflammation, promote brain health, and provide an excellent supply of vitamins A, B-Complex, C and K.

FAMILY

Red Bean Quesadilla

Ingredients

½ cup red pinto beans, drained and rinsed
¼ cup cubed onion
¼ cup cubed green bell pepper
1 garlic clove, minced (or 1 teaspoon garlic powder)
Pinch of chili powder or cumin
1 tablespoon olive oil
1 tablespoon tomato paste
1 sprig of cilantro
Salt and pepper to taste
¼ cup shredded Monterey Jack cheese
Flour or soft corn tortilla

| | PREP TIME 10 min | COOK TIME 20 min | WATER Level 3 |

Steps:

Put the beans, onion, green pepper, and garlic in the steamer basket.
Pour water into the tank (level 3).
Start the cooking process.
When the bean mix is cooked, put it in the blending bowl and set aside the cooking liquid.
Add olive oil, tomato paste, cilantro, salt, pepper and some of the cooking liquid to the bean mixture and pulse to a chunky consistency.
Spread the bean mixture on tortilla. Sprinkle cheese over the top. Fold tortilla in half.
Cut into triangle portions. Or toast in a non-stick skillet over medium heat until cheese is melted, being careful not to burn tortilla and cut into triangle portions.
Serve immediately.

🔍 *Foodie Fact*

Red beans are full of fiber that helps lower cholesterol.
Add the optional cumin to help aid in digestion.

FAMILY

Butternut-Cheddar Mac and Cheese

| ⌣ PREP TIME 10 min | ◷ COOK TIME 10 min | ◌ WATER None |

Ingredients:

1 recipe Creamy Butternut Sauce
recipe *(page 71)*
2 cups cooked elbow pasta
¼ cup grated cheddar cheese
¼ cup breadcrumbs

Steps:

Mix the butternut sauce, pasta, and cheese together in a bowl.
Scoop into Béaba Multiportions Silicone tray, top with a sprinkle of breadcrumbs and bake in preheated 350° F oven for 5 to 10 minutes to warm and brown breadcrumbs.
Serve immediately. You may also store in a Béaba Multiportions Silicone tray refrigerated for up to 3 days.

🔍 *Foodie Fact*

A healthy alternative to regular mac and cheese, this dish sneaks in butternut squash, which is loaded with vitamin A and C.

FAMILY

Tahini-Miso Sauce

Ingredients:

1 tablespoon white miso paste
½ cup sesame tahini
Squeeze of lemon juice
1 tablespoon maple syrup, agave, or honey
1 to 2 tablespoons water

Steps:

Put all the ingredients except water in the blending bowl and blend well until it forms a thick sauce.
Add water and continue to blend to desired consistency.
Store in Béaba container in refrigerator up to 4 days. It will thicken in the refrigerator; add water if needed and stir before serving.

🔍 *Foodie Fact*

Miso is a fermented food, which aids in digestion. It's a great addition to dressings, sauces and stir-fry recipes for its added umami flavor, which brings depth to savory dishes.

FAMILY

Salmon and Sweet Potato Cakes with Tahini-Miso Sauce

PREP TIME
15 min

COOK TIME
40 min

WATER
Level 3

Ingredients

2 ounces salmon fillet, skin removed, cubed
1 cup cubed sweet potato
¼ cup breadcrumbs or 1 tablespoon coconut flour

1 egg white
Pinch of garlic powder
Pinch of cinnamon
Pinch of chili powder or cumin
Pinch of salt and pepper

1 tablespoon olive oil
1 tablespoon butter

Steps:

Preheat oven to 350° F.
Put the salmon and potatoes in the steamer basket.
Pour water into the tank (level 3).
Start the cooking process.
When salmon and potatoes are cooked, remove to a bowl and cool. Discard cooking liquid.
Put the cooked ingredients in the blending bowl and add the egg white, breadcrumbs, garlic powder, cinnamon, chili powder or cumin, salt, and pepper. Gently pulse 2 to 3 times. Remove to bowl again.
Chill in the refrigerator 15 to 30 minutes.
Scoop one tablespoon of salmon mixture at a time and form into small cakes.
Heat the butter and olive oil a non-stick sauté pan over medium heat and pan-fry the salmon cakes about 1 minute on each side until golden brown. Remove to a parchment-lined baking sheet.
Bake in oven for 10 minutes.
Serve immediately with Tahini-Miso Sauce (page 111). You may also store in Béaba storage containers up to 4 days refrigerated or freeze.

Foodie Fact

Salmon is loaded with Omega 3 fatty acids that help maintain insulin levels, improve brain function, and maintain healthy skin and hair.

FAMILY

Banana Walnut Pancakes

PREP TIME
15 min

COOK TIME
40 min

WATER
None

Ingredients:

¼ cup oats
2 tablespoons flour or vanilla protein powder
1 tablespoon ground flaxseed or ground chia (both are optional)
1 teaspoon baking powder
Pinch of cinnamon
Pinch of nutmeg
Pinch of salt
½ cup sliced ripe banana
1 egg
1 tablespoon coconut sugar or brown sugar
¼ cup milk
¼ cup chopped walnuts
1 to 2 tablespoons butter or coconut oil

Steps:

Put the oats, flour or protein powder, ground flaxseed or chia, baking powder, cinnamon, nutmeg, and salt in the blending bowl and pulse a few times to combine. Remove from bowl.
Put the banana, egg, and sugar in the blending bowl and blend.
Add the milk, walnuts, and dry ingredients in alternating additions, pulsing in between until batter just comes together. Do not over mix.
Heat 1 tablespoon of butter or coconut oil in a non-stick skillet over medium heat so oil just coats bottom of the pan. Spoon batter into skillet. Cook gently about 2 minutes per side (batter will form some bubbles).
Remove to a paper towel lined plate. Serve with maple syrup.
Serve immediately. You may also store refrigerated for up to 4 days.

Foodie Fact

These tasty pancakes are loaded with oats to boost energy. The walnuts also provide good Omega 3 fats that can help lower cholesterol.

FAMILY

Chocolate Olive Oil Cookies

Ingredients

½ cup semi-sweet or dark chocolate chips, divided
¾ cup flour
¼ cup cocoa powder (unsweetened)

1 teaspoon baking soda
2 tablespoons olive oil
1 egg
3 teaspoons coconut sugar
1 teaspoon vanilla

½ teaspoons coarse sea salt (optional)

PREP TIME
15 min

COOK TIME
10 min

WATER
None

Steps:

Preheat oven to 350° F.
Melt ¼ cup of chocolate chips in a saucepan on low heat.
Put the flour, cocoa powder, baking soda, in the blending bowl and pulse to combine.
Remove to a bowl.
Put the olive oil, egg, coconut sugar, vanilla, and melted chocolate in the blending bowl and blend.
Add the dry ingredients and extra chocolate chips and pulse just until batter comes together.
Scoop 1½ tablespoon-size dollops of dough onto parchment-lined baking pan. (Option: sprinkle tops of cookies with coarse sea salt before baking.)
Bake for 10 minutes.
Cool on pan.
Serve immediately. You may also store covered for up to 3 days.

Foodie Fact

Dark chocolate helps regulate blood sugar, lower cholesterol and boost immunity. Olive oil makes these cookies a super, heart-healthy treat.

FAMILY

Coconut Oat Lactation Cookies

PREP TIME
15 min

COOK TIME
15 min

WATER
None

Ingredients:

½ cup almond flour
1 cup oats
3 tablespoons coconut sugar
½ teaspoon baking soda
1 teaspoon cinnamon
½ teaspoon sea salt
2 tablespoon brewer's yeast
(to aid in lactation for breast
feeding)
2 tablespoons coconut oil
2 tablespoons ground flaxseed
mixed with ¼ cup hot water
(flax "egg")
¼ cup raisins or chocolate
chips

Steps:

Preheat oven to 350° F.
Put the almond flour, oats, sugar, baking soda, cinnamon, salt and brewer's yeast in the blending bowl and pulse to combine.
Add the coconut oil and flax "egg." Pulse to combine. Dough will be dense.
Remove dough to a large bowl and fold in raisins or chocolate chips.
Scoop 1½ tablespoon-size dollops of dough onto parchment-lined baking pan. Gently flatten cookies with palm of your hand.
Bake for 15 minutes until golden brown.
Cool on pan.
Serve immediately. You may also store covered for up to 3 days.

Foodie Fact

Brewer's Yeast is highly nutritious and full of iron, protein, B vitamins, and other minerals. When combined with oats and flaxseed it helps boost milk production in nursing moms.